Weaving my Spiral Outward

Poetry and Prose Shaping Landscapes of Soul

Geneviève Nolet

To Annemarie ♡,
May you find pieces
of yourself between the
lines. May your perceptive
& gentle spirit be supported
by the art & poetry -
— thank you for reminding
me of my talents -
Only love & light
♡ 2011

ISBN **978-0-557-44607-0**

Dedication

This collection of poems is dedicated to Chris Gour (1946-2002), witness and mirror, with whom I began my journey on the mending path of love~ Now a loving voice, forever present in the gentle spaces between everything.

Foreword

I have known Geneviève Nolet for many years, and have been astounded, again and again, at her amazing resiliency and the intense clarity of her perception of the inner life and how that life unfolds. As long as I have known her, she has been pursuing "the unveiled beauty that lies beyond the ego," (The Golden Pathways), remarkable in itself in one so young. That is what appears in this collection.

The "faint, shimmering strings" of her inner life are visible, here, both in image and in word. For Genevieve's gift is for both expressions – writing and painting – and they are equal in their power and their invitation to the reader and viewer to look into the mirror of their own lives in this exquisite collection.

In this book, you are being given both heart-breaking and heart-healing visions. They arise from such a depth in Geneviève that they are universal: any of us can detect our own faint shimmers of resonance in the offerings of this work. Geneviève's dedicated attention to bringing into light her own "pieces" invite us to consider our own, and she illumines the path to that possibility.

Feast your eyes, minds and hearts here. This is the primal journey, that daily paradox of life, the "making soup" of relationship, the chance to "dampen our own armour." And to come – but in peace, at least for a moment, - to "rest in the center of the world/still knowing nothing."

Thank you, Geneviève, for your courage and attention, your fidelity to your own voice and vision, and your gift to the world that is this book.

Brenda Peddigrew, Ph.D.
SoulWinds, Halls Lake, ON
April, 2008

Preface

"Our songs travel the earth. We sing to one another. Not a single note is ever lost and no song is original. They all come from the same place and go back to a time when only the stones howled." (Louise Erdrich)

Our songs do not ask of us to be perfect; instead they require tenderness and bravery, precise vigilance and the ability to listen in order to fully embrace the gifts they hold and to liberate them into the world where they can dance unbound in magnificence with the divine. For many years now, dancing my way through love's labyrinth, I have come to know that the journey is one of weaving through the spiral, forever returning to the beginnings with new insights and clearer visions, but nonetheless a journey of retracing steps that I never thought possible, uncovering new ground. This collection of songs is merely a reflection of my soul-weaving as my spirit persists to awaken and dive deeper into truth, into knowing, into love.

"...as you strode deeper and deeper
into the world,
determined to do
the only thing you could do-
Determined to save
the only life you could save."
(Mary Oliver, "The Journey")

The words have been and must continue to be consistent companions, honest mirrors and reliable friends on this winding path towards self, towards heart. The lessons that rise and fall between the words are lessons of the soul. They are personal portraits of my inner life. They are at times the trembling voice of truth that dares to ask the difficult questions or that pours light into the darkest of nights and, at other times, oceans of unwavering bravery.

"There must be
in the dark
pieces of me
that hold the knowing
that it isn't so!"

(From "Pieces of Me")

"As I dive in
I decide that if I spin downward into the spiraling vortex forever
then at least I will have dared to live
if only for an instant
(From "What I Fear Most")

The words that sing themselves into this collection were born to be shared in the hope that they may illuminate and offer solace. I offer them in love and in light. No matter what their message, they wait for your willingness "to save the only life you could save."

Table of contents

Chapter 1
The Golden Pathways

"You are here to enable the divine purpose of the universe to unfold. That is how important you are!"

(Eckhart Tolle)

So I rise now. Out of the sleep. Out of the unawareness — once again — feeling a hypocrite, know nothing, ready to face the life that mends and shapes as fluid as the sea...

I describe the flow of my life between the lines in hope
to trace a path, familiar and circular...
the path that heals and awakens...

This is why I am Here —

The Golden Pathways

I keep thinking
what if I were to write it all down?
The inner stirrings
the awakenings that transpire in my own life
in my heart really

The walls that break down
The layers that shed
like old skins peeling off bones
The ephemeral moments of clarity and peace
that suspend all molecules of emotion
Those few moments when everything makes sense
and all is right, as it should be

Yes, all of those miracles
that continue to scar my human flesh
What if I were to write them all down?
So that someday
Someone
Somewhere
maybe could be found by it
and found in it

What if the only words that spilled out of my mouth
were only the truths of my spirit, bare?
What if?

And so I take a vow
to honour and recount the intrinsic movements of my being
To witness the true nature of my nature unraveling
and write it down

I vow to let creativity rise in and out of me
and onto the white pages

I vow to engage in my own magnificence
and let light shine through
infusing the edge of my dark

I vow to seek in others
the unveiled beauty that lies beyond the ego
and evoke the magic inherent
within the kindness we all truly hold
I vow to remember that all we really want is love

Past the bones that frame me
these truths leak into my flesh
and braise my spirit raw
I recount the unraveling of the universe
shaped over the last million years
as if I had been part of it
present in some way

I know I was
There is no other explanation
that could justify this inner knowing
that seeps in and out of my flesh
and glimmers there
full and faithful

The pulsating atoms of my spirit
recount all of those days
In reverence
I acknowledge the gifted generations before me
who continue to shape the universe
by their active participation
in the unfolding of atoms and space
and who relentlessly
shine forth luminescence
that conquers every heart and every dark
Luminescence that enfolds whole
the golden pathways of truth

...Deep past the bones that frame me—

My Divine

I am reminded of what really matters
I reconnect
over and over
with the divine
My divine

Nothing in the world can take away the meaningful
My life's purpose is to continually propel myself into the abyss
Further into the unknowing

I want to be a clear voice
An honest voice
surrounded by the ego that prevails

Today
I remember the truth of my life
and I am empowered by those gifts

I have been too tired to remain conscious
but in this safe and heavenly castle
I return to the roots
I return to love

I return to love

The Truth of You

The brilliant truth of you~
Traces of your life
dispersed beneath
unraveling eternal carpets of stardust

A still picture in time~
You came
a vision
tired from journey
away from everything I had ever known

Quietly

Snow falls
Quietly
Covering grounds
Covering me

I fall
Quietly
Uncovering grounds
Uncovering me

Consequence (for B.P.)

"I don't think you take your art seriously enough!"
The truth of her words
resonates deeper
as the day begins to fade out

My drive back
through autumn's edges
of the Haliburton country roads
softened my hard edges
The artist
cries herself to sleep every night
as my heart swells with knowing that the true humbling thing to do
is to give her space to breathe

I am so blind
limited by my own sense of self-preservation
There are endless possibilities

The gifts
will continue to plague me
brave
and
relentless
until my body
can no longer battle against
the significant currents of truth
that throb in my veins

And so
I must carve enough space
out of the dark restrictions
that deplete the light
from my heart~
Until it knows to beat
slow, full, strong and true

The truth of her words...
Consequences that seep into flesh
birthing riches

The Only Life I Would Ever Want to Live

I just got back from an art show.
It amazes me, every time,
how many brave souls there are out there,
showing up with more baggage
than the strongest camel could ever endure.

Setting up with the hope of maybe selling one piece of art for more
than $200 out of a whole display that took more than 10 years to
build…
The choices on every table,
the many transformations all there,
exposed for the world to see.

The crowd infiltrates the space slowly at first,
but every single person that passes through gets changed.
They may not make the food bank donation
but they get changed.
They walk by,
they read some words,
they get lost for a fraction of time into colours, shapes, their
meaning…
They shift physiologically.
There is a brain-heart-spirit connection or the sudden awareness of
a disconnection
But there is an impact~
Suddenly someone gets changed.

I sit there
beside my art table
and make an evening full of connections
without saying a word.
I make slight imprints of paper money
but I receive instead,
the gift of being witness to the world meeting mine.

All night,
I see people seeing themselves in my work.
I know at that exact moment,
this is what I am meant to do.

I sat close to the table all night.
It was magnificent.
It was magical.
Not my work but the reason for my work...
Every single person had a response...

Some just walked by or through,
as if on a mission to dispel and repel,
making every attempt to miss everything,
while the corner of their eye tried to capture everything in a flash.
They wear their discomfort all over their clothes.
I take the deep breath they try to hold.
Some spent over 15 minutes reading through,
holding their hearts and walked on,
as if reminded of who they are.
Some looked totally confused
but still had that look in their eyes
that whispered silently
that they knew more than they let themselves believe.
Some were kindred, truly unveiled.
The supporters with paper money were kind and centered...
on the road of the golden pathways I am sure.

The room was crowded by 8:30.
Every voice began to beat to the sounds of the background band.
It was a nice band.
Only two people actually, an acoustic guitarist and a singer.
I tried to make conversation
as I saw him take his guitar case out of his little white car from Meadowvale.
I see a guitar and I get all soft and heavenly,
I can't help myself.

Well it didn't matter, he was not in the mood to engage,
or so it seemed to me.

Anyway, I sat beside my table
and I felt like I was almost part of the walls, the floor and the air in the room.
It was a good place to be.

Then the night wrapped up.
It was over...
I looked at my list of sales and my heart sank from underneath itself,
actually, further than that!
It sank and folded,
it caved in
deep.

I tried to hold the tears back.
I think a few came out against my will.
Throat tightened
I swallowed the rest.

I hear the real words around me now.
People talking at me.
I am wrenched from witness and quickly,
I am very much the artist who needs to start packing up her art display,
and load her car with almost everything she arrived with.
It is the end of the night.
Between the artists' jokes,
talking about this and that and the way it is,
my heart folds and twists.
I know to be grateful,
but I refuse to think that this is how it is.
Because I have a dream
and I don't have to listen to the lies we tell ourselves.
Artists are not broke.
Artists don't have to die in order to become worthy.

True, artists do make an ultimate sacrifice: the true giving of themselves,
the drudgery of honest hard emotional, spiritual and physical labour
of birthing the gifts back into the world,
in darkness and in light.

But I refuse to fall into the belief of scarcity
because I know that artists are plentiful,
of a different and magnificent currency, at least.
Those gifts brushed my right cheek all night long by my art table.

In a beautiful paradox, the sadness visits me late tonight.
Morning work calls out.
I ask for space for just a few more lines…

I know this is who I am.
I know that it is all I want to do.
And I know that I am more vulnerable than I ever knew I could be.
I know that I lost $300 in supplies alone.
But for the first time,
at the age of 34,
I finally know that I can no longer pretend to be any other.
I write this last sentence down
and the cleanest tears fall heavy on my writing table,
my heart busting open.
The truth resonates past Mars
and hits my flesh hard on its way back,
reverberating.

I know that I take the biggest risk of all
to fall deep into the bottomless abyss
cradled in the arms of blinding truth
To lose everything…
Myself…

I also know that the road through
the road out
or maybe the road in
is a series of spiraling in and out of the path,
in and out of confusion,
with much hard work, more sacrifices and no mercy
but there is just no one else I can be.
I have resisted the truth of who I am since before I could walk.
Actually that fear is what almost killed me once
17 years ago
half my age exactly
I knew then
what I know now
that I could never be any other.

Just got back from an art show...
Changed
Richer
Holding hands with the only life I would ever want to live.

Isn't It?

This is impossible I thought....
How would I ever live the life my heart desires?

The truth is-
as death brushes against my eyelashes
day after day...
I continue to feel
the pang of truth pulling me in
but the unanswerable questions
spin me further away from myself

Perhaps the only way to satiate the need
is to loosen my grip once and for all

Perhaps there are no answers
to these questions~
Perhaps,
the simple life I lead is exactly enough!

Perhaps there is nothing more to do
than just let the truth spill out
every day~
For no other reason
than to honour my choices to live honestly
That has to be enough~
That is enough~

Perhaps it is only the love
I feel undeserving of
that I constantly look for
But isn't it right here?
Buried deep into my chest?
Isn't it right here,
Pounding?
Boisterous?

I am saving my
life. The deeper
one. Deep between
each of layers.

The mist
lifts once more,
as it always
does - I am

steady.

Chapter 2
An invitation

"Your task is not to seek for love, but merely to seek and find all barriers within yourself that you have built against it"

(Rumi)

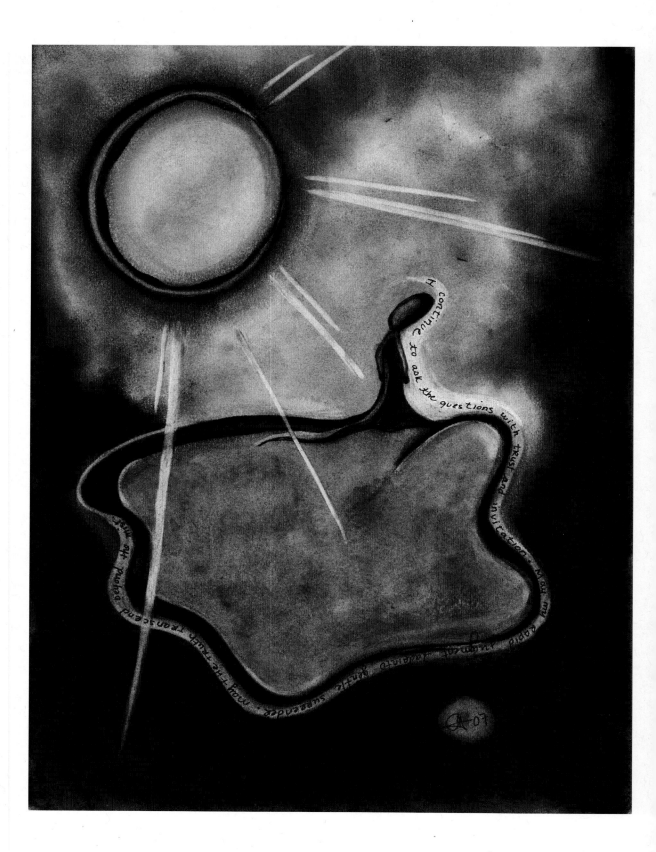

Trying

In the obscurity
you could find me
trying to imitate the sound of what my voice would sound like
if it only learned to speak

Flooded

The wind is strong here
The sun comes out for an instant
it beats into the ripples
of a once calm lake

I am taken to a place I barely remember
I begin to wonder
but the clouds
too eager to cover up
steal the fast fading memories
The sun fights back though
and pierces through the opaque sky
straight through my morning skin

In a sharp moment of light
I am flooded with imprints
perplexed images
that too quickly fade away
like sand through fingertips

My pen
much slower than nature
finds it difficult to encapsulate the thoughts that may come
So, I forgive the pages and move
instead
towards breakfast

I Miss Her

I look at myself
Age three
Magnificent smiles in the bathtub

My eyes lock into hers
I swear she can see me

We both know she holds
the sacred wisdom of the child
I miss her

With No Love

Dancing in the arms of the debate team
I sit in my car
as anger rises from unknown depths
and rushes to my throat
My eyes begin to bulge out from their sockets

I sit here in my car
with the rebellious child
who feels
unheard
unseen
with no love
and with feelings
too unfamiliar for her to comprehend

I Can Hear the Subconscious

The stories of sick babies
getting all the attention
pulling mothers away
Sick people did not have to feel aloneness
they had moms

I hear the messages of the subconscious
I know healing is inherent~
The messages...
There is attachment
however absurd-

I hold on to the need
as the endometriosis
the appendicitis complications
and seasonal allergies
wrap themselves up into living things
and converse with my every cell

I am my subconscious...

There Will Come a Time

Hostility also drags behind
leaving a trace of irritation on my breath
I speak not of the anger between my teeth
but hold on tightly
to a tale I can barely masticate

Instead
I keep walking along the windy path of transformation
with a faint shimmer of trust
that there will come a time
when I will be strong enough to hold
both the sadness
and piercing anger

There will come a time
when I no longer
silence the terror
and let out the scream

Fantasies of a Better Mother

I return home
kick off my platform boots
Run a hot bath
I slide in
just long enough to fill the tub with water
Just long enough to warm my body
My cold body

I find a pen
a piece of paper
and lay on my bed
undone
like these sheets and blankets
all twisted up and falling off the edges

In my warm pyjamas
I take a deep breath and begin to untangle the deep secrets
The secrets I hold on to with dear life
The secrets I bury
in the deep of my belly
tightly kept in isolated confinement
far from my breath that can no longer reach

I sit
unveiled
uncensored
with emptiness
twisted bed sheets
and the fantasies of a better mother

The Gift Lingers On

"I will be your Juniper"

and the gift lingers on
like a damp blanket over fermenting grapes
like a dead leaf on my favourite plant
not ready to let go just yet

Just a Little

My legs feel stronger
deeply rooted in both
truth
and disenchantment

The illusions
thick like midnight fog
lift
clearing paths
softening hearts

The wounded child
was acknowledged
She breathes deeper now

And so
in me
she begins to trust
just a little

No One to Hold

Something is missing
or at least unfamiliar
like I lost something
or found something I don't recognize
My life in transition is strange
There is no restful place

I go through the day
because I have to
I have no desire to engage in conversation
and I have relinquished the need to fix it

I go through the day
with her smile around my heart
and the gift of the other
sitting on my chest
beating rhythms of unconditional love

I hope for the storm to fade
and eventually break into shards of transformation
Unfortunately
my sky continues to fill with opaque dread
The wind blows unfamiliar
and nothing breaks into rest

I just sit in the middle
with no one to hold
and no one to tell the stories
I barely understand myself

In my Body

In my body
tears rise to the top of my sternum
I clench my teeth
in an effort to dismiss
The tears collect the pieces there
and form pockets of vulnerability under my sleeves

My shoulders
curl under my breasts
protecting my wounded heart
I take a shallow breath
in an effort to dismiss

From beneath me
history rises to my knees
I lock my gait
in an effort to dismiss

I am consistent in my effort to reject
I hold away
at arm's length, the softening I know~
The softening which will move me
to the deep
the rich
and the divine
I hold away
I hold

The efforts elude me
and my resilient body returns to its rhythm
It pulls me into its cadence
It pulls me into the pockets of vulnerability under my sleeves
Into history that rises to my knees
and into my wounded heart
I try so hard to protect

Truly Missing You (to C.G.)

The sky and water collide into shades of gray~
The day after the storm
A few sail boats and motorboats waltzing on the surface
A single duck
floating around
neck sunk deep into its feathers
altered by each wave
just floating along

I connect with nature-
Colours faded
Lines blurry
and much of no movement
but tiny waves hitting the rocks below
stirring the pollution and moss into an unappealing green soup
Dull colours~
No shine~

This incredible sadness without its usual sharp edges
throws me into a state I wish I could ignore
and the duck floats my way
sleeping perhaps…

Yesterday's reprieve
comes to an end this morning
and envelops my skin~
raw and bare~
Like the lobster shedding its exoskeleton
on its way to the depth of the sea
I, too, am searching for a rock to cave under
but instead
I float
like the duck
riding the waves
in search of you

It is really the in-betweens that haunt me
The places between highs and lows
Between the ripping and rejoicing
The before and after the chaos or the peace
It is the place
suspended
in suspension
which causes me to ache
Like this discomfort that seeps its way beneath my skin
between the grief gripping and the tears that won't come

I think of my mother-
A family of ducks has now joined the landscape
Ten of them floating about
awake now
as the waves accelerate and break into the gray
I think of my mother
I accept her experience
as a child into a woman's body

I sit on the rocks
writing about my journey
and the too sudden loss of you

The truth is still wrapped into a blanket
which I carry around my waist
like period cramps
but I keep writing in an attempt to stay connected to it
and with shadows of her
blowing in the wind

Pockets of peace wrapped in shards of chaos
too prickly for me to hold~
The anxiety flowing free in my veins
barely covering up the grief
that collapses breaths~
That falls heavy into lungs~

My life today
At this particular moment
Bold~
Intense~
Lonely~
At this particular moment
truly missing you~

I wonder when it will be enough~
When will the truth be freed from my waist
and dance in the sky
within the gusts of you?
Where are you?

My Bare Feet Acknowledged They Had Known Nothing Else

Sleepiness crawls under the covers
and plays like a cat with my toes
I pull away
not ready to give in
not ready to play dead
not yet

My toes find a comfortable place
safe from its prowl

My bare feet acknowledge
they have known nothing else
besides the long, weary, treacherous road of today
filled with panic and shame

My eyes blinking
at the verge of surrender
now curl into my pillow
just before the dream

Pieces of Me

Is it possible for me
to exist if no one sees me?
Can I believe
without the world reflecting me
that there is
still
someone to see?

Why must I only find truth
if the world tells me so?
How can my experience
not matter
without the mirror?
How can that be?
It isn't so!

But it sure feels that way
Spinning here
alone
unseen
unheard
unaffected

There must be
in here
in the dark
pieces of me
that hold the knowing
that it isn't so!

The Only Road

If only I had lower self standards
If only I did not care about my spiritual evolution
then I could be unwilling
to fall into those depths

Sometimes
I fantasize
of being dumber than dumb
or in just absolute denial

But soon enough
I come to admit
that the only road towards my heart
is one that requires precise awareness
forgiving presence
and brave vigilance

What I Fear Most

Is it my existence
to continually fall into the void
that is made of me?

I have no other questions
No answers
Simply the impulse to fall in at once
and let myself drown deep
into that endless pit of nothingness
and spin there
forever

There is no other part of me
that resists what I fear most
forever falling in the pitch black
of nothings and everythings and "I don't knows"

Alone
without the net that is you
Alone
and never really finding anything there
but a heart that grows cold and weary
eyes no longer adaptable to light
and no love

Just much too much
of too much empty

As I dive in
I decide that if I spin downward into the spiraling void forever
then at least I will have dared to live
if only for an instant

Chapter 3
Dark Dance

"....the endurance of darkness is preparation for great light."

(St. John of the Cross)

Haunted

The day flirts with despair
as I ride the morning subway
The stories fail me
but the ache sinks its way into the bone marrow
Beneath my skin
the frame that barely holds
trembles

In the dark tunnels
between stations
I stare at my empty reflection
in the flashing windows
searching for the good mother
The images that come back at me
are complicated distorted pieces of history
I barely recognize
or understand

These images
haunt me
for days on end

A Premonition

The sharp edges that cut and wound
Screams in the dark
The prison of past horror

The ripping of what was left
The piercing shriek

The affliction resonates
reverberates in my bones
It disfigures

The sharpness
The attack
Days before the damage was done
A premonition

Why

I dared to dream and found my body forever asleep
My hands touched the sun and now I bleed
My eyes saw the truth and now I cry
And I still am wondering why

Falling

I fall
Deep
Deep beyond the usual darkness
Deep past the gifts
Deep into the truth of defeat

It slips away
the trust

There is deep sorrow
There is hurt
Unexpected hurt
The kind that shatters

My heart breaks
The howling sound it makes
pierces my diaphragm
ravaging my insides

I fall
Deep
Deep beyond the usual darkness
Deep past the gifts
Deep into the truth of defeat

You

Sometimes
You is just the part of me that cannot sit with the self
You as a figure of speech
and also at times
the voice of the one who knows
The one who asks of me
what I have asked her
to ask of me

Without You

As I am here
without you
falling into the abyss
that spins me silly
I realize how much of a net you are

But if, once again,
the gift is to fall
deep
deeper
deep into the void that spins
and spins some more
then maybe,
being here
is really what precipitates the plunge
and then,
I remember everything

Without you for days
that feel like years
I am here
without you in between

I understand but I can't stand it
that place you wish for me to dive into
It scares me there
No one is there
Just me with my new skin
my exposed flesh
and the dichotomy of nothings and everythings

Where you want me
without you I can't stand it
She evades me
Her strength fades

I am here
without you
falling into the abyss
that spins me silly

The Agony of my Own Presence

Pushed out of the nest
Here I am
in this all-encompassing solitude
isolated
with only the subtle and frightening movements of my inner life

So I come here
and try to be true
as true as I am
and maybe someone will let me know that I am not going mad
Maybe then I will hear
the words that will help me to sustain the agony of my own presence

Maybe then
I will be able to stand
feet planted into my own being
and know that there was always love

All l I Have Are my Words

All I have are my words
My words
The words
They are my only friends

Right now they are the only ones I can trust
The words
are what I have

There is just no one else here
but me
in this soupy mess of a life
that bubbles up to the surface
that raises its angry fist

My sweet love is so sick
growing through a transformation
that requires all of her
I love her
I miss her
Our life disintegrates without her

And all I have is my language
My precious written language
that pours out so fast
I can barely keep up

I cannot be mindless
I am paying attention against my will
I can see everything
It hurts
The truth hurts
But what is the truth?
What hurts in the truth?

I write it all down
completely overcome by what comes
The clarity and the confusion
sharp like a knife on both accounts
in the same day
or more than once in a day
I ask the questions and they come and they fall and I fall
and I stand and I fall and I stand and I fall and I stand
all at once in the same day

All I have are my words right now
because the one who listens is sick
the one who knows is away
and the one who understands
well
she scares me

All I have are my words
The most unbearable metamorphosis I have ever lived through
and all I have are my words

But I am grateful for my words
The secrets between the lines
The natural progression of intention
The sweet momentum of truth

The entire day I spend
suspended
waiting to come back here
where my heart can fall back onto itself
within the words

The words that guide, that mend,
that push me forward,
that replace the mentor
who decides she wants
"that little bit that's left"

All I have are my words
between every tired breath
that manages to make its way out of my chest
and into the world

The Dark Forces of You

The dark forces of you
spread their thick black
over my chest
There is barely enough room to breathe
I resist the resurrection of your annihilating presence
with every breath I cannot take
The sound of drums
barefooted dancers
screaming around the burning fire of fury
I hear their beats louder and louder
Now
It is all I hear

The tidal wave takes me under
still I resist
You ugly, loud, all-encompassing angry woman
Who are you?

I wish to silence those screams
I wish to silence my tears and my thoughts
I wish to silence you
I wish to never let anyone know the racing bleeding drums of fury
I wish to never be
Never be
She

The Pyjamas You Refuse to Slip Into

I am not sure where you have gone
Lost somewhere between the bathroom
and the pyjamas you refuse to slip into
The light in your eyes
completely fades
Your trance-like sway
Your incomprehensible words
Your inability to hold the treasures in your hands
Your long dragged-out painful chews
Where have you gone exactly?

I fight with you all night
I wish I did not
I try to keep my mouth shut
for minutes at a time
but those minutes are so long
they tear flesh off my bones
if that is even possible

I am not sure where you have gone once again
but the process of watching you disappear
slowly
one part at a time
seems just too much to bear
My heart cracks
My tears turn into shards of salt
and all I can do then is yell at you to go to sleep
so that maybe
tomorrow you will return to me
full of your usual grace with treasures and light in your eyes

Enough Room for Both of Us

I was raging for three days
unsure really of where it was coming from
but the fury ravaged inside and out
I felt trapped inside my own body-
with nowhere to go
breaking

Trapped between two undesired outcomes
two dead-end options
I fell victim of a story I could barely masticate
No one told the truth
There was nowhere to go
nothing to do, but to rage some more

At some point yesterday
between another furious spin
and an unwelcome shutdown
the truth started to spill out
brave and clear
untainted

She finally slipped into her long-awaited pyjamas
She sleeps this morning
no longer denying the truth that plagues her
With it comes along reprieve, forgiveness,
space for me to grieve… to change

I stand, early with the sun
ready to prepare the arrival of my clan
expecting nothing more than for her to let go
to bathe in the arms of recovery
However long it takes, as long as the truth keeps spilling out

The fury fades into the night
and leaves in its path enough room for truth
enough room for both of us
The force that ravaged me
restless and cunning
held tender secrets that mend
In the end
we return to love

Avalanche

No sleep
and life swings a series of full plates
in the kitchen of my days
The sink is full
I am running out of hot water
but there is no reprieve
no more dish soap and
the full plates keep on coming at me

Beneath this chaos
there is calmness and a laugh
that allows me to ride through
this avalanche of bugs
this rising anxiety

A laugh
without which
all of this would be
unbearable

Belly Up

My mind continues to melt
and I sit in the middle of the puddle
with a blank stare behind my eyes

I navigate the waters without a map
Thankfully my body floats

Someone may find me
belly up
in a starfish configuration
holding my melting brain towards the sun
as I gaze into the optimistic vision of a good night's sleep

Tonight I Ask for It in my Dreams

Confusion
The waters
murky
The nights
moonless

How is it
that I come to know
everything at once
and also
can't seem to see
anything at all?

When will I know?

The descent into the void
seems endless
Never any ground

There are moments
when my feet are flipping around
as my hands search frantically
for a hold
and others where I am free-falling
into the comforting silent echo

When will I know? (I ask)
Well at least I no longer ask why

I know this for sure~
That there will come a time
when every part of me
will know
by the sound of my cellular fabric
dancing into YES

So
I try to put to rest
the desire to be somewhere I have not yet arrived
and embrace my way
through the descent

There is only one thing left for me to do
So tonight
I ask for it in my dreams

Long Enough Reprieve

There may soon
be nothing left
for me to find
between the lines

I write the words down
to make my story
truth
recorded
but also to pause,
deliberately slow down the process

It is as if
closing the book,
the written truth,
somehow makes it better
It softens the blow
Offers reprieve

Just for a little while
until the currents
pull me back under
where I fall deep

I now, then,
put away the pages
and hope for a long enough reprieve
that will mend and strengthen
before it is time to return

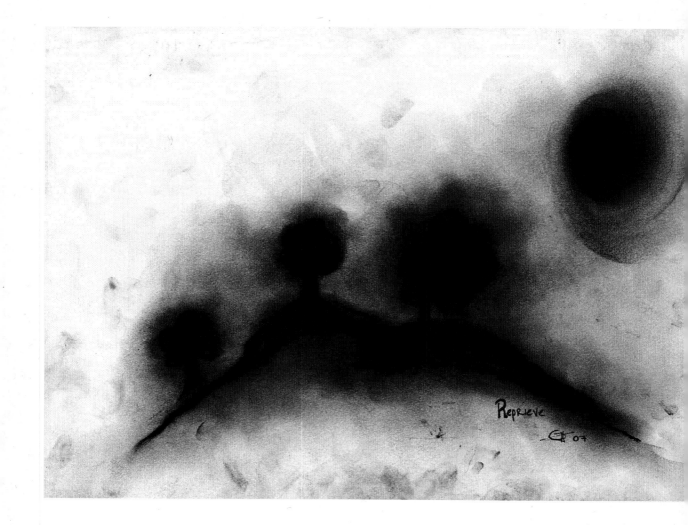

Chapter 4
Befriending the Shadows

"You are experiencing the tender wound of life itself. It is where we must all go and in slowly bearing the feelings, dwell ourselves. It is what makes us strong, loving and creative. This is to be celebrated and we will!"

(Brenda Peddigrew, Ph.D.)

The voice that guides so much stronger now as I give her words to speak, Feet to dance so - in both her strength and

she rises from the depths of my belly and electrifies my senses as she bathes her fluidity into every cell supports my BONES

RE-ENTERING THE NEGLECTED BODY, I breathe in the dying of the old skeleton. My skin sheds layer after layer & exposes the raw flesh of the ragged dolls. Soft spoken/clear & sharp, the dolls tell a tale of burning houses - of intruders & of magical forests. I am invited inward on a hike through the mis-shapen, mis-placed and mis-aligned. I find there - between the trees - hidden clearings & poetry. It is there that the skeletons & ragged dolls meet the tender wound.

03

Within the Dream

I continue to dive
into the dream of my days
often mistaking them for my life
I continue to walk through the hidden clearings
with night sweat on my lips

I am unsure of these times
for all my images are blurred
all my shapes distorted
and my songs
interrupted

I no longer search for a hold
I just allow for the suspension
to exist
within the dream

The Turbulent Molecules (for J.W.)

I make the brave decision to sit
to breathe through the racing heart
the shortness of breath
the pulse deep and above my eye

I courageously bring my intentions
towards releasing the frantic vibrations
through
and out of my body

I sit here
in full sun
in my driveway overlooking the wise robust shed
that takes its place there
proud and sturdy
between the garden
and the car spot

I sip on lemony water
I loosen the grip
I release the vibrating
turbulent molecules
and open the door
I let them out of their constricting envelope

The internal buzzing slows down
It slows down enough for me to hear
the sound of my own voice

How do I heal my heart?
What dark layers must I remove?
How do I regain my birthright to homeostasis?
Where do I bring my body to rest?
To vibrate with ease and rest-full-ness?

I can almost hear the answers
whispering between the empty spaces
of each unwritten line
like a rumble of true
glimmering in the dark
I hear them
I know them
With my own eyes
never have I seen them
but these truths are in the spaces between everything

I throw my fishing rod into the universal pond
and wait for insight to bounce against my ends
and pry my mind open long enough for me to notice
and let it settle in my bones

I have no other plans
I am white canvas
willing to be honest

I made the brave decision to sit
to breathe through
the racing heart
the shortness of breath
the pulse deep and above my eye

I courageously brought my intentions
towards releasing the frantic vibrations
through
and out of my body

I am now
the unwinding path
of turbulent molecules

Into the Vortex of Love

Inside my heart
there is a place
that holds words I barely know

I observe my heart quivering
Free-falling into the never-ending
vortex of love
Speechless

I come to know (most of the time)
that there is strength in my bones
Strength bigger than me
that holds this fragile frame

I hold gently
so as not to crush
the love that burns my spirit
and hope to continue to hear the voice of truth
that resonates into the deep echo of the universe

Softly at First

It expands
all around
I find no rest
The discomfort is painstaking and reliable
smooth like chamomile tea

The deep ache is now but a faint throb
that bounces on the surface of my resilience
I greet it half open-hearted
The wounds propel me further and further into myself
where for the first time
I find refuge
Refuge from the great dark

I am tripped into a cascade of unfamiliar freedom
as night crashes into this bedroom window
I choose to stay here
without her
The tears finally come
softly at first
and then
nearly sobs
This momentum washes my face clean

Shadows of the void emerge through the night
I want to run away
back home
Get into my car that does not start
and drive back to my comfortable prison

But I don't~
I couldn't~
Instead, I cry until the sobs turn into tears
and the tears turn into sighs
and the sighs turn into stillness

Now I sleep
Soft and restful
with visiting kitten who decides
over and over again
that my bed is a gigantic scratch post

Stillness & Tears

Reshaping Landscapes

Waking from a nap
at the tender time of three
Bright noon
long gone now
The snowstorm stealing away
the fast-fading sun
of shorter days

Still
traces of antibiotics running through
making me so very sleepy
offering in return vivid dreams
lingering about for hours past the rest
reshaping landscapes

In the corner of my eye
intricate shadows dance their invisible tango
They disappear as soon as I look straight at them
They offer no reprieve
They make it difficult
to re-enter the world unaffected

Misshapen, I stand, fragile
unaware of their full implications
but almost ready
to expose
the unwelcome truth
that seeps through the layers of denial
and disrupts my comfortable standstill

Who Are We?

The sadness in your eyes this morning
A mirror of my own desolate condition
The love in my heart burns down the frame that barely holds
Still I wish for us so much more than this

The sound of your steps crashing crisp into snow
as you leave towards the day
eyes on the ground
shoulders wrapped around your chest

Images of you
falling over feet
as if walls shifted position
without you noticing

I stand by the door
seeing you disappear into morning sun
hoping for love to reach your heart
and soften your convoluted layers of worry and pain

Images of me
Falling into holes
as if on a road never traveled
unable to dislodge

I sit in the middle of truth
noticing self disappear
wishing to blind the eyes that see
so as to not have to choose

The sound of my breath breaking through brittle gusts
as I enter another day
Eyes misty
Turning away
Body bruised from harrowing wind

The grief in my chest too soon to untangle
Witness of stories untold~
Beyond the love that binds
who are we?

Spilling

I rise out of the glass
past the bubbles
past the ice cubes and the lemon

I rise out of the glass
and begin to spill
onto the kitchen table
where I once held on too tightly
in fear of empty spaces
and nourishing voids

I spill onward
onto the white pages of thoughts not yet thought of
I spill
and slide off the edges of comfort
where I find little pieces of me
scattered but intact

And I spill some more
I spill enough to make my mother proud
even then
I spill some more

And the more I spill
the more I see
The more I see how much of me
there really is to see

Tripping

Tripping
as if by mistake
into my own steps
Establishing
a rhythm of my own

In the Dark

I stand still
in the middle
in the dark
The spaces around me idle

The anxiety no longer scares me
but it spreads its oppression
in the dark
It infiltrates my lungs in an attempt to suffocate

I stand still
I breathe through
There are pockets of freedom
budding in the dark

My entire day
halted
in the dark
hovering

I am still here
amidst the blurry lines
the out of touch
the hazy eyes

I am still here
suspended
in the middle
in the dark

I breathe deeply
I fold within
I hold with tenderness
I meet you in the dark

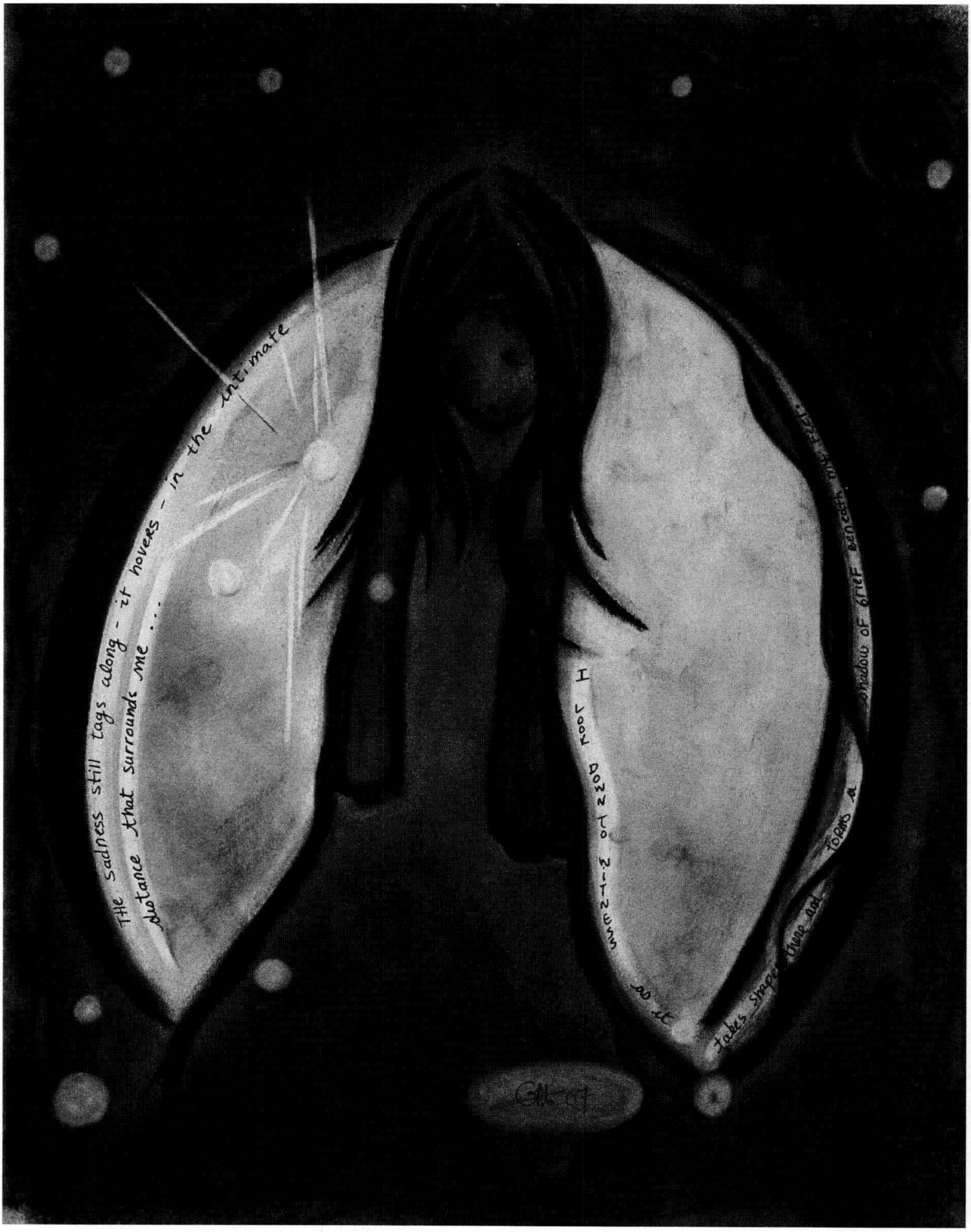
THE sadness still tags along - it hovers - in the intimate
distance that surrounds me . . .
I look down to witness
as it
takes shape there and
forms a
shadow of grief beneath my feet.

Mending

I sense in the air
the mending
bubbling to the surface
as the witch stirs
her giant bowl of green stench

She is dedicated to the process of making magic
out of all that is ugly and smelly
I am grateful for her vision
for she brings to the surface a tale of transformation

Her fearlessness to incorporate
and embrace the perilous
the unsightly
is fascinating

As the heated soup bubbles over
with messy
foul
and wicked honesty
I can only hope to be blessed
with the same vision of truth

I leave her cabin,
out into the deep woods of my soul
where I find my magical tree

I rest there
undisturbed
mending
waiting for truth to reach my heart
and melt away the thick layers
of empty space and fear

Hovering above the Vortex

Cold November morning
I try to keep warm with my big hooded sweater
but the chill in my bones is resilient
I feel trapped between the cold that wraps its way around my flesh
and the fog that spreads thick over my heart

I am tired
but there are swirling forces beneath that fatigue
that twist my spirit
I circle fast
above the vortex
unwilling to plunge deep to its centre
trying to hear the words
that spin me deaf

there is faint recollection
of spirit
of heart
of knowing
They too
spin the vortex
I am reluctant to wed

I lose my way
The lessons fall off like old skins
still I am pulled in
closer

Hovering above
suspended
at the edge of knowing
The birds chirping in the bare lilac tree
outside my window
remind me
I bare witness to the mystical truths of One

I can almost hear the words now
layered between the emptiness
layered against my resistance to change

There is love
There are endless possibilities
There is power
There is a law
without judgment

There are signals
deeper than thoughts
at the core of beliefs

Words felt and embodied
that fling my life open in abundance
or infertility
every day in this channel
There are choices
accountability beyond measures

The work feels hard today
I let myself off the hook
My resistance shall breathe
without my added contempt

There is only one thing left for me to do
to sink
deep
into the center of chaos

I am the spinning vortex
fatigued
reluctant
deaf
but
brave

Beneath the Dark Polluted River

I have opened my heart
in gentle spurts
Perhaps there is still more truth to surface
from the deep guarded fortress

I find some forgiveness
but much disappointment
perhaps my guarding apprehends a loss
I am unwilling to process

My heart aches
confused by the lingering defeat
that rolls heavy
at the bottom of the well

I vowed to be gentle presence
to the lessons that rise and fall
from the poison
of my contaminated waters

There is love
beneath the dark polluted river
I sink in it
to the mucky bottom
befriending the shadows
of which I am made

Chapter 5
Finding the Resting Place (Weaving my Spiral Outward)

"…to the finding of that which is lost and to the mending of that which is broken.
Blessed it be, it shall be so."

(Monica Furlong from "Juniper")

Busted Open!

An explosion of light
Sharp shards of truth
breaking open my spirit
like a watermelon
with black seeds all over my face
My pupils no longer brown
they are mirrors

An explosion of true
that shatters even the ground under my feet
There is no longer
anything
I am free-floating
in the middle of a sweet-fruity-pink ocean
with black seeds all over my face

I am the ruins...
I am here...
Busted open!

Negotiating the Paradox

My wings feel heavy
pulled and sore
tired from the journey
from the deep
The light
almost too much to bear…

The love that permeates through flesh and gentle bones
pierces my resistance (sometimes)
There is also difficulty in re-entering the world
changed
transformed
mended (at least some parts of me)

There is difficulty in negotiating the paradox
Difficulty to wear the many skins I am known to be
They fall off
I negotiate with difficulty
and then
somewhere in the middle of this dance
the struggle to integrate lifts (at least a little)

I am here without the too many masks that made me me
Without the protection
the illusion of safety
the stories I tell myself in order to survive
Without the lies that somehow have become my friends

I tuck my tired wings under my breasts
offering them rest
grieving the loss of another layer
as I prepare to negotiate some more

I Think So...

A thought…
Maybe truth pierced my spirit
Maybe there is inner peace
for an instant
Maybe nothing matters,
and everything does
Maybe everything is perfect
inside of me

Inside of me
that inner being
full of light
It soothes
like a gentle buzzing
a hum

Could I actually be coming into my own being?
Greeting my own self
at the edge of my ends?
Could I have been…
this entire time?

Could there also be an unbreakable core?
Some kind of everlasting shimmering nucleus
that cannot be shaped
or influenced by anything?
I think so~

Maybe I surrender~
Surrender to the loss of this layer
falling off
like an old coat
heavy and worn out
one that has matured
into a beautiful, soft, lived-in favourite

This new layer is thin
not worn for long enough
I can sense my body-electric right at the surface
vulnerable
still free-falling into the abyss
with incomprehensible restfulness-
I know that I know nothing

But I am sure that I know this
Someone new is here
She has been here for a few weeks now
long enough for me to notice
She brings along a love I never knew
One I have been searching for
all of my life
in all the wrong places

Her arrival is timely-
As everything always is-

Could I really be her?
I think so...
I think so!

If I Think So...

If I think so
Then does it make it true?
If it makes it true than what does it mean?
Who visits me now then?
Besides the unsettling sensation of newly-exposed bones?

If my purpose is really to be She in me
then I really know
that I know nothing
But also everything

Then I know both the incredible emptiness
that rises like heavy tide
and also inner presence
that softens everything

Presence that softens everything
The truest of all true things
The absolute absence of fear
The impenetrable strength of surrender

On the other hand and all at once

Emptiness that rises like heavy tide
This utter aloneness that rips at the core
The bring-you-down-to-your-knees kind of heavy
That thick mist of uncertainty

Who visits me now then?
I search for answers between the lines
inside the words
within the sharp vulnerability that sits on my chest
I search everywhere so that I can maybe find a way to integrate
She
in my body

I ask myself...
If it is true that She is me
then why does it matter?
I am here
visiting me!

Beyond Flesh and Bones

She
in me
easier to see
is recognizable now

I witness light hover
over everything she touches
A clarity of language
that expands beyond usual comfort
Present to the microscopic movements
of the energy that bears the mystery

There is ease about her
A kind of calm
An impenetrable love
She arises from the depths
the great depths
with a knowing
that speaks no language

I re-enter the world
I plunge into my heart
I dive in
head first
arms open

I return to essence
I realize that there are forces
beyond my own flesh and bones

Parasympathetic Dance (for T. D.)

The day unraveled
into the hands of the magician

Cradled by the hands of the universe
for an instant
deep plunge
transforms into nourishing hover

I go on and on
through the expansion and recoil
through the spiral of life
through love's labyrinth

I let go
with intentions
Fear no longer overpowers
it just whispers without consequence
The too many masks fall off at last

I lean back into the gentleness of my spirit
arms across the breath of my belly
muscles soaking into their parasympathetic dance
heart open

Can We Be Saved?

I can hear the world
rumbling
echoing

There is movement deep under the sea
where the fishes
in their last attempt to share the lessons
create ripples
the size of tidal waves

Whatever you say
The centre of the earth bubbles to the surface
It squeals
with a piercing shriek that blinds
The world is falling apart
as I sit around
in a stupor
lost in a pool of blood

Presidents without intentions
Without forecast
Without truth
Without accountability

I can hear the world
rumbling
echoing
There are wars
Wars that scar the soul
There are wars
Wars that disfigure humankind
The truth stares us down
unafraid
waiting

Little children in their splendour
killed by the hands of ignorance
Are we forever lost in greed?
Greed for a liquid that ravages our existence?

I can hear the world
rumbling
echoing
This incredible sense of doom
slips its way between my good intentions to inspire
and my attempts to shift the world around me

I am consistently reminded of the rumbles
at the center of all truths
that shake the very foundation of my existence

I give way to the alarming messages
in my body
that unveil the covert annihilation

Will you engage with me?
Will you participate?
Will you hear the piercing shriek?

Making soup (for A.W.)

I keep talking about how much I want to write with some context… Instead, I make organic chicken soup for my darling (not a bad alternative). I begin to prepare the mix for the magic cauldron. Garlic, onions, bok choi (a fabulous green vegetable that she swore she did not like before she moved in with me). Actually, she was adamant that she did not like vegetables. Especially asparagus and avocados… Now she buys them at least 3 times a week. She was so funny. Her fridge must have contained $250.00 worth of packaged, processed, bleached food items I thought people didn't really eat in public or even in the closet anymore. "WonderBread," sugary peanut butter, processed cheese and all sorts of cookies and snacks. To tell you the truth, I loved it. When I slept over, I found reprieve from the laws of good health for at least 12 hours.

Just like when I celebrated my 8th (or was it my 9th) birthday… I can't remember. I got to have a bucket of Kentucky Fried Chicken with my best friend. It was more like my first date EVER. Kentucky Fried Chicken and a date with a girl… Though no one else knew it was a date, not even her… (perhaps I did not even know myself… at least consciously!) but what else could a 4th grader wish for… It was heaven! I still have a picture of myself from that night. Wearing the weirdest shade of purple ever purple shirt tucked into my dorky jeans so far past my waist making my entire torso disappear. What were we thinking in the 80's? Were our parents trying to protest the decadent fashions of the 60's and 70's? Standing as far away from the organic hippy bell-bottoms as possible? Fashion at its worst! When I see shadows of the 80's in my students' outfits, I get invisible aneurysms and pseudo-seizures. My body goes into total fashion trauma. I know most would disagree, but please… leg warmers and skinny bottom jeans!!! I scream quietly in my head and hope that this too shall pass. In retrospect the 60's and 70's were great years, at least from the sounds that seep out of my old picture albums, with similarities to the 2000's I have to say: the rage against Presidents, music that breaks down the walls, the anti-war movement, the save-the-planet coalition, the deep knowing that all we really need is to love one another! In the picture from my 8th birthday, I am leaning over the counter, hiding with all my might the discomfort of a young girl's crush: the truest happy face ever, hiding behind a bucket of Kentucky Fried Chicken!

Back to my darling though… I have to say in her defense that there were always some potatoes and lettuce in her over-filled fridge, and let us not forget pickles and baby carrots (her veggie salvation) or sometimes maybe a bunch of broccoli and sun-dried tomatoes that would be assembled when she would make her famous "I want to go to bed with you tonight" delicious chicken pasta dish. It always worked. It was good. We would always stay up late. I am getting further and further from this chicken soup though! I want time to write but I am making soup. Now I add to the cauldron couscous, lentils, homemade chicken stock, carrots, celery, olive oil, spinach, crushed tomatoes, curry-pasted chicken pieces boiled away from the carcass from the night before… All steeping on the stove for hours…

Amy eats now
and
I
come
here
and
try
to
write…

Maybe I could write like Hollywood Farm Girl… you know… with some context and let the style describe who I am. I love that… She is brilliant! To be able to incorporate clear storytelling into art, that is an accomplishment, and to actually take the time to craft life onto paper, wow! …to stop time and let the true internal dialogue of how I experience life unravel without any interruptions, without any thoughts of anything else being more than what really is. No poetry – no premeditated or analyzed metaphors. No thesaurus. Just the roll of the thought as it is. No interruption between words and thoughts. No little debate between the thoughts I don't want to have and the ones I wish I had. Me! Nothing else! Bare~ Naked~ Fearless~ No thesaurus for a more appropriate word that would better describe the thoughts. What a concept!

I resist. I think perhaps because English is my second language, I don't get to write an entire entry without my thesaurus... After all, I am French. French people get to look up words, don't they? Words in English seem much more appropriate though... I have to say I often wonder if maybe I was English-speaking in another life. The question falls off... My first language, French! Are you kidding me! I could never write in French. I remember in grade 9... (In Montreal it was called Secondaire 3. We had grade 1-6 as Primary school and then we graduated to high school called "Secondaire" where we took grade 7-11). The look on my face I must have had when I realized that I may have to repeat my third year of high school because of French class. I didn't get it. The crazy French grammar insanity! Really. Who designed that language anyways? A table is feminine and a kitchen counter is masculine? What do you mean you have to put an "er" at the end of a verb and not an "ée" when I use the verb "to have"? What??? French grammar was my nightmare. Punctuation was another problem... though perhaps I still struggle with that one...

This is it! My first real uncensored entry ever! It is nearly 9 PM now... Time to taste this soup and catch the new episode of my favourite TV show~ Besides, I did manage to write an entire entry without the thesaurus!

Happy eats~

Good night~

Peace out~

To the Magic

I speak my words with as much honesty as I am capable of
I do it because I have to
I need to
It is the best thing I can do

I search deep under the layers
where I find truth
The energy that has no judgment
That knows without fear

I am here because I want to
In the middle
connecting with intentions
finding magic

Grateful that I saw you
You stood, undeniable
My Achilles heel
My Trojan princess

There is a soulful sister
who, time after time
from her own journey returns to the roots
and takes a moment to engage with the most moving presence

And then you came
with vulnerable gentleness
There is a light in you
that shines beyond all shame

The other who slips in and out of utter presence
The one who dances with the magic
but keeps it far enough
that she can become separate

There is the sister...
The mother... The wise child
The reincarnation of willingness
The beautiful, strong and engaging brilliance

There is the woman warrior who converses with the angels
Love as consistent as my breath
The child in a woman's body
Who lives at the root of all healing

There is solidity
The kind of sturdiness that grounds
Full of grateful and ease
You navigate through time with splendour

There is simple loving kindness in you
A calming presence that reassures
An honest desire
Reliable and grounding

There are muses who engage with the power of intentions
The ones who remind us of what really matters
The singer with accountability
The one who chooses life day after day

There are moments of complete harmony
Moments with words that comes from beyond the mind
Moments with spiraling stillness
where everything makes sense

There is the man
The boy... who embraces fatherhood at last
The kind of love that was always there
The kind of love that always saved me

There is true dedication, true Vision far away in another country
brilliance at its best prospers in a lab somewhere
between lack of sleep and long hours that last forever
she is the kind of family that I cherish

Once upon a time there was a roommate
The kind everyone wishes they could have
The loyal friend… with consistency and clear intentions
that guided me through the very dark

There is the young sorceress
The one with miraculous hands
She is filled with so much soul
The kind of perfect
She is paying attention

There is a luminous smile that permeates every cell of her being
A woman who continually recognizes the magic in others
She holds the gentle heart of Chris
She makes a mark
There is ripple

There is the magician… The mentor…
The one who reminds me of the sacred
and of the undeniable truth that beyond the mist
love always prevails

I am so blessed
I am grateful for all the lessons
For the chaos that gives birth to grace
For cradling my spirit in the eye of the storm

Thank you
Today is a day to remember the light that shines
beyond the layers
where there is magic!

My Dampened Armour

My outward life gets hectic so fast
The buzzing, busy of city, of new millennium
of work harder, longer
to make more money
to buy over-priced houses
over-priced clothes
that have traveled all around the world and back
to save the corporations a few pennies as they mindlessly
in some sort of stupor
abuse whole nations for less than a dollar a day

To buy over-priced cars
that leak over-priced fluid
and ravage our mother

Our mother... incest survivor
Despite the terror that churns her roots
she continues to spin the world
and cradle us without judgment
But for how long?
We pose the question
and we go on blinded by this abuse
busy
abusing

The empty, fast-paced rhythm replaces the full throb of meaning
with ego that splits us at the roots, that turns us into living ghosts
walking around the earth in hopes to acquire
more
faster
longer
to over-produce and consume
more than we could ever chew

I hear the words tumbling around my head
like the clothes in an overfilled dryer
bumping around
too tightly confined to get enough air to dry

My thoughts
crowded
formless
blobs of damp

I manage to take a few items out
and leave the others with more room
for the possibility of a chance
to tumble more freely
and birth
from their back pockets
the buried gifts they hold

If only I could manage
a bit more time

The list of things to do grasps at my throat
and tightens
further and further

Work!
Harder!
Longer!

I pry the hold open
in hopes that it may be enough to let out
just a few meaningful words
but my words are empty
my thoughts
soggy

I remember though
that for every insignificant word
that echoes past the shame
deep in the dark abyss of creation
The possibility for space to exist is offered
Isn't it there?
Deep in the void that I am made of
where the forces who bear everything
nurture the sacred and the divine?

If it is so
then perhaps
my ridiculous use of the English language
and my seemingly empty conversation
within the words
may light
some love
into the dampened armour
I wear
in the meantime

When the Time Comes

Panic sets in as I hang up the phone
The truth of this situation
is by far
the last thing I wish to face
but the most profound
and urgent task at hand
One that requires much gentleness
intertwined with precise power, strength and foresight
Without it
nothing is possible
for either of us

I come to regret
for an instant
the commitment I made to myself
years ago
to never go back
To never let myself disappear
To never choose easy over true
To never walk blindly with a shattering heart
To never walk the path of willingness
with an unwilling participant
who wishes with all their might
that they could want to

The heaviness
sits on my heart
I look towards
in an attempt to appease
the torturous discomfort

I remind myself
that nothing else matters
However afraid
I am at an impasse
I take responsibility for the light of my spirit
I promise
that when the time comes to choose
I will choose to live
I will choose life

Yes

I am grateful to know
that beyond the ego
that gives birth to fear
there is an unbreakable core
that awaits our direction

Today
Let us reconnect with yes
and be reminded that there are no gaps we cannot close
That if we all danced our way into our hearts
the world would be a magnificent place

Enough

A wound heals
Despair lifts
The heart opens

There is less fear
Easiness
More truth

A wound heals
and the space it creates
leaves an opening
I never thought I would be capable of

There is peacefulness
Rest
There is finally enough
There always was enough!

Well-Traveled Moments

I have been there and back and there again
I have visited my darkness
my childhood closet
my emptiness
my fullness
my mediocre self
my abundant self
my intensity
and my numbness

I have seen the changes
the metamorphosis
I have witnessed my recoil
as love touches me

I have witnessed child
brilliant
wounded and forgiving

Friends holding
seeing
dying

I have seen the nature of my nature
unraveling

I return home from the well-traveled moments
but I remind myself that I will return
Go back to the haunted
the spirited
I remind myself that I am intact
That in facing death I was awakened
That in touching darkness there was light
That in connecting with the deep ache in my belly
succulence emerged

I remember the paradox
forever present in the "in-betweens"
for I will return to the dying
the wounded
and the fearful
I will return to the shedding of old skin

Until then
I will continue to awaken
and embrace who I have been
who I am
and who I am becoming
respectfully

Treading Gentle Waters

My commitment to stay connected
through the dark
yielded gifts
beyond my imagination

And so I return
to a state of fragile balance
with traces of collapsing breaths
and ghostly imprints of adrenaline rush in my mouth

The budding freedom
blooms in its splendour
I am here
treading gentle water
Determined to Fly

In a sparkle of dust
dropping from the sun
she swoops me
complete

Like a love soldier
slipping through time
she wakes inside of me
in a million shivers
an ocean of sweet tingles

Her voice
unmistakable in my dreams
later dissolves
into delicate intuition

I step into the light
with raindrops on my breasts
spreading my wings
determined to fly

Flawlessness of True

There is a gentle rhythm in my cellular fabric now
It radiates through every layer
It begins to expect
undeniable commitment from me
I let it
because I have come to know that the cost is much more otherwise

I witness
as she thrives rightfully
relentless
confident
and clear

There is a newfound willingness
to be bare or even ridiculed
judged
misunderstood

Along the path towards ourselves
the profound dichotomy of ego and heart
forces us to trust
in our absolute refusal to compromise the nucleus
It keeps us mindful
Courageous

There is the sweet sound of truth
and for each time we let it rise
bones settle
our diaphragm pulls in enough oxygen
every breath we take sinks in a bit deeper
our spine realigns

The full rumbles of the heart
tell us that we are exactly where we should be
and that for each day that goes by
we can begin to believe in who we are becoming

Everything falls off
The path clears
I look at the momentum of one molecular right
Its impact on the whole is significant
It leaves us intact
powerful
tender
interconnected

Courageous becomes easier with practice
or perhaps
the transformation it yields
motivates
and propels us deeper into the flawlessness of true

Weaving my Spiral Outward

The waves
weaving my spiral outward
whisper ever so slightly
that rest comes

I let go of the hold
I rest in the center of the world
still knowing nothing

About the Author

Blessed with determination, dedication and a love of healthy living, Geneviève has founded her own massage therapy practice in downtown Toronto. She has been teaching in the massage therapy and spa assistant programs at her alma mater, Centennial College, and assisting on occasion the research department at the College with ongoing research projects. Geneviève Nolet is a writer, poet, artist, teacher, massage therapist and dancer. 17 years ago, she moved to Toronto from Montreal to pursue a career in modern dance. Knowing only a few words of English, through persistence and with the help of many, she has taught herself the English language and has been residing in downtown Toronto ever since. She finds pleasure in cooking fabulous meals for her friends and family, is slowly learning to play guitar and is deeply inspired by music. Her journey has always been on the road towards truth and heart and in honouring the intricate inner movements of the soul.

Her heartfelt gratitude goes to:

Her family for their love and willingness to heal;

Chris T. for his fabulous editing work and his refreshing sense of humour;

Nathalie (who fuelled the young writer), Kristina (truest of true artist and friend who understands this magic. May she embrace her gifts that she knows are magnificent! She inspires!), Sarah F. (for having eyes and a heart that really sees and a spirit that smiles and illuminates the world she touches), Marta (who always supported the artist from the very beginning), Amanda (for being one of the first to hang Geneviève's art on her walls and for being a true lover of poetry-meets-art), Candace (for her consistent loving presence), Marybelle (the muse in magic and music), Antony (the young boy with wise eyes and a pure heart), and the many wonderful souls who have inspired her in one way or another over the last 34 years of her life;

Natalia, young goddess and wise beyond her years, who inspires (every day) to choose brave over easy. A true soul sister, companion along this journey toward truth and who cradles the words ~ whose love for grammar and syntax rescued this book from itself;

Brenda Peddigrew, healer and writer. Mentor and spiritual guide, who is a consistent mirror and a tender voice, who makes much of this journey an inspiring and miraculous process, and for being a driving force in honouring the self with tenderness and bravery. Heartfelt thanks for her own dedication to truth, for having the courage to speak her words. They are true, tender and propelling;

Her dear friend Mary, attentive listener, magician in her own right, who always believed that all of this was possible;

Melissa Etheridge, the singer with accountability, who awakens the activist and who fuels dedication, inspiration and hope, who mesmerizes and awakens. Who will always be her true muse in love, in heart, in truth and in art

And Amy, gentle-hearted, patient, generous and unfailing witness to the words — to this part of the journey.